Fav
Prayers

Catholic

Classics

Edited by

Rev. Victor Hoagland, C. P.

Illustrated by

William Luberoff

THE REGINA PRESS
New York

Artwork © Reproducta, Inc., New York 1996
Text © The Regina Press, New York 1996

Table of Contents

Guardian Angel Prayer

Angel of God,
my Guardian dear,
to whom God's love
commits me here.
Ever this day
be at my side
to light to guard
to rule to guide.
Amen.

Prayer to Saint Joseph

O St. Joseph, whose protection is so great, so strong, so prompt before the throne of God, I place in you all my desires. O St. Joseph, help me by your powerful intercession, and obtain for me from Jesus all spiritual blessings. So that, having engaged here below your heavenly power, I may offer my thanksgiving and homage to the most loving of Fathers. O Saint Joseph, I never grow tired contemplating you, and Jesus asleep in your arms; I dare not approach while he reposes near your heart. Press him in my name and kiss his dear head for me and ask him to return the kiss when I draw my dying breath. Amen. O Saint Joseph, hear my prayers and obtain my petitions. O Saint Joseph, pray for me.

This prayer was found in the fiftieth year of Our Lord and Savior Jesus Christ. In 1505 it was sent from the Pope to Emperor Charles when he was going into battle.

Whoever shall read this prayer or hear it or keep it about themselves, shall never die a sudden death or be drowned, nor shall poison take effect on them; neither shall they fall into the hands of the enemy, or shall be burned in any fire or shall be overpowered in battle.

Say for nine mornings for anything you may desire. It has never been known to fail.

Feast Day: March 19

Act of Consecration to the Sacred Heart

Merciful Jesus, I consecrate myself today and always to your most Sacred Heart.

Most Sacred Heart of Jesus I implore, that I may ever love you more and more.

Most Sacred Heart of Jesus, I trust in you!

Most Sacred Heart of Jesus, have mercy on us!

Most Sacred Heart of Jesus I believe in your love for me.

Jesus, meek and humble of heart, make my heart like your Heart.

Prayer to Our Lady of Perpetual Help

O Mother of Perpetual Help, with greatest confidence I present myself to you.

I implore your help in the problems of my daily life.

Trials and sorrows often depress me; painful privations bring heartache into my life; often I meet the cross.

Have pity on me, compassionate Mother.

Take care of my needs, free me from my sufferings or, if it be the will of God that I should suffer still longer, grant that I may endure all with love and patience.

Mother of Perpetual Help, I ask this in your love and power.

Prayer to St. Jude

(To be said in cases despaired of)

Saint Jude, glorious Apostle, faithful servant and friend of Jesus, the true Church invokes you universally as the patron of things thought to be hopeless; pray for me, who am so miserable; pray for me, that finally I may receive the consolations and the aid of Heaven in all my necessities, tribulations, and sufferings, particularly *(here make your request),* and that I may bless God with the communion saints throughout eternity. Amen.

St. Jude Apostle, martyr and relative of our Lord Jesus, Christ, of Mary and of Joseph, intercede for us.

Family Prayer

God made us a family.
We need one another.
We love one another.
We forgive one another.
We work together.
We play together.
We worship together.
Together we use God's word.
Together we grow in Christ.
Together we love all people.
Together we serve our God.
Together we hope for Heaven.
These are our hopes
and ideals.
Help us to attain them,
O God, through Jesus Christ
our Lord.

Prayer to
Our Lady of Lourdes

O Immaculate Virgin, mother of mercy, health of the sick, refuge of sinners, comforter of the afflicted, you know my wants, my troubles, my sufferings; look upon us in mercy.

By appearing in the Grotto of Lourdes to Saint Bernadette, you were pleased to make it a privileged sanctuary, whence you dispense your favors, and many have already obtained the cure of their infirmities, both spiritual and corporal. I come, therefore, with the most unbounded confidence to implore your maternal intercession.

Obtain for me, O loving Mother, what I request *(here mention your request)*. Through gratitude for your favors, I will endeavor to imitate your virtues, that I may one day share your glory.

Our Lady of Lourdes, Mother of Christ, you had influence with your divine Son while upon earth. You have the same influence now in heaven.

Pray for me; obtain for me from your divine Son my special request if it be divine will. Amen.

Prayer to
Our Lady of Fatima

Most Holy Virgin, who appeared at Fatima, to reveal to the three little shepherds the treasures of graces hidden in the recitation of the Rosary. Inspire our hearts with a sincere love of this devotion, in order that by meditating on the Mysteries of our Redemption that are recalled in it, we may gather the fruits and obtain the conversion of sinners, and *(here name the other favors you are praying for),* which we ask of you in this Novena, for the greater glory of God, for your own honor, and for the good of souls. Amen

Our Lady of the Rosary of Fatima, pray for us.

Prayer to Our Lady of Czestochowa

(To be said each day upon arising)

Holy Mother of Czestochowa, you are full of grace, goodness and mercy. I consecrate to you all my thoughts, words and actions; especially my soul and body. I ask for your blessings and especially prayers for my salvation. Today, I dedicate myself to you, good Mother, totally; with my body and soul, amid joy and suffering, to obtain for myself and others your blessings on this earth and eternal life in heaven. Amen.

Prayer to
Our Lady of Mt. Carmel

Most beautiful flower of Mt. Carmel, fruitful vine, splendor of heaven, Mother of the Son of God and Immaculate Virgin, assist me in my hour of need. Star of the Sea, help me and show me that you are my mother.

Holy Mary, Mother of God, queen of heaven and earth, I humbly ask you from the bottom of my heart, to assist me in my hour of need. There are none that can withstand your power.

Show me that you are my mother. Mary, conceived without sin, pray for us who have recourse to you. *(3 times)*

Dear Mother, I place this cause in your hands. *(3 times)*

Feast Day: July 16

Prayer to
Our Lady of Guadalupe

Our Lady of Guadalupe,
mystical rose, make intercession
for holy Church, protect the
sovereign pontiff, help all
those who invoke you in their
necessities, and since you art the
ever Virgin Mary and Mother of
the true God, obtain for us from
your most holy Son the grace of
keeping our faith, sweet hope
in the midst of the bitterness
of life, burning charity and
the precious gift of final
perseverance.

Feast Day: December 12

Prayer to Saint Thérèse

Saint Thérèse, the Little Flower of Jesus, please pick a rose from the heavenly garden, and send it to me with a message of love.

I beg you to obtain for me the favors that I seek *(here mention your request)*.

Recommend my request to Mary, queen of heaven, so that she may intercede for me, with you, before her Son, Jesus Christ.

If this favor is granted, I will love you more and more, and be better prepared to spend eternal happiness with you in heaven.

Saint Thérèse of the Little Flower, pray for me.

Prayer to Saint Michael the Archangel

Saint Michael the Archangel, defend us in our day of battle; protect us against the deceit and wickedness of the devil. May God rebuke him, we humbly pray.

And you, O prince of the heavenly host, by the power of God, banish into hell Satan and all of the evil spirits who roam through the world seeking the ruin of souls. Amen.

Prayer of
Saint Francis of Assisi

Lord, make me an instrument of
your peace.
Where there is hatred,
let me sow love;
Where there is injury, pardon;
Where there is doubt, faith;
Where there is despair, hope;
Where there is darkness, light;
And where there is sadness, joy.

O Divine Master,
Grant that I may not so much seek
To be consoled as to console;
To be understood as to understand;
To be loved as to love;
For it is in giving that we receive;
It is in pardoning that we are
pardoned;
And it is in dying that we are born
to eternal life.

Feast Day: October 4

Prayer to
Saint Anthony

Saint Anthony, gentlest of saints, your love for God and charity for his creatures, made you worthy, when on earth, to possess miraculous powers.

Miracles waited on your word, which you were ready to speak for those in trouble or anxiety.

Encouraged by this thought, I ask you to obtain for me the favors that I seek *(here mention your request)*.

The answer to my prayer may require a miracle, even so, you are the saint of miracles.

O gentle and loving Saint Anthony, whose heart was full of sympathy, whisper my petition into the ears of the infant Jesus, who loved to be held in your arms; and the gratitude of my heart will ever be yours.

Feast Day: January 17

Jesus, I Trust In You!

The Chaplet of the Divine Mercy

(For private recitation on ordinary rosary beads)

Our Father...., Hail Mary..., The Apostles' Creed.

Then, on the Our Father beads you will say the following words;

Eternal Father, I offer you the Body and Blood, Soul and Divinity of your dearly beloved Son, Our Lord Jesus Christ, in atonement for our sins and those of the whole world.

On the Hail Mary beads you will say the following words:

For the sake of his sorrowful Passion have mercy on us and on the whole world.

In conclusion three times you will recite these words:

Holy God, Holy Mighty One, Holy Immortal One, have mercy on us and on the whole world.

(From the Diary of the Servant of God Sr. Faustina —Note Book I, p.197)

IMPRIMATUR: + Joseph F. Maguire
November 17, 1979 Bishop of Springfield, Mass.

Novena of
Childlike Confidence

(This Novena is to be said at the same time every hour for Nine consecutive hours—just one day)

O Jesus, who said, "Ask and you shall receive, seek and you shall find, knock and it shall be opened to you," through the intercession of Mary, your most holy Mother, I knock, I seek, I ask that my prayer be granted. *(Make your request.)*

O Jesus, who said, "All that you ask of the Father in My Name, He will grant you," through the intercession of Mary, your most holy Mother, I humbly and urgently ask your Father in your Name that my prayer be granted. *(Make your request.)*

O Jesus, who said, "Heaven and earth shall pass away but my word shall not pass," through the intercession of Mary, your most holy Mother, I feel confident that my prayer will be granted. *(Make your request.)*

Prayer Before a Crucifix

Look down upon me, good and gentle Jesus, while before your face I humbly kneel and with burning soul pray and beg you to fix deep in my heart lively virtues of faith, hope and charity, true contrition for my sins, and a firm purpose of amendment.

While I contemplate, with great love and tender pity, your five most precious wounds, pondering over them within me and calling to mind the words which David, Your prophet, said of You, my Jesus:

"They have pierced my hands and my feet, they have numbered all my bones." Amen.

The 23rd Psalm

The Lord is my Shepherd;
I shall not want.
In verdant pastures He gives
me repose;
Before restful waters He leads me;
He refreshes my soul.
He guides me in right paths for His
name's sake.
Even though I walk in the dark
valley I fear no evil;
for you are at my side,
with your rod and your staff
that give me courage.
You spread a table for me in the
sight of my foes;
you anoint my head with oil;
my cup overflows.
Only goodness and kindness follow
me all the days of my life;
And I shall dwell in the house of
the Lord for years to come.

The Lord's Prayer

Our Father,
who art in heaven,
hallowed be your name;
your kingdom come;
your will be done
on earth
as it is in heaven.

Give us this day
our daily bread;
and forgive us
our trespasses
as we forgive those
who trespass against us;
and lead us not into temptation,
but deliver us from evil. Amen.

Safely Home

I am home in heaven, dear ones;
Oh so happy and so bright!
There is perfect joy and beauty
In this everlasting light.

All the pain and grief is over,
Every restless tossing passed;
I am now at peace forever,
Safely home in heaven at last.

Did you wonder how I so calmly
Trod the valley of the shade?
Oh, but Jesus' love illumined
Every dark and fearful glade.

And he came himself to meet me
In that way so hard to tread;
And with Jesus' arm to lean on,
Could I have one doubt or dread?

Then you must not grieve so sorely,
For I love you dearly still;
Try to look beyond earth's shadows,
Pray to trust our Father's will.

There is work still waiting for you,
So you must not idly stand;
Do it now, while life remains,
You shall rest in Jesus' land.

When that work is all completed,
He will gently call you home;
Oh, the rapture of that meeting,
Oh, the joy to see you come!

Saint Dymphna

Lord Jesus Christ, you have willed that Saint Dymphna should be invoked by thousands of your believers as the patroness of nervous and mental diseases. You have brought about that her interest in these patients should be an inspiration to and an ideal of charity at her great shrine and around the world. Grant that, through the prayers of this youthful martyr of purity, those who suffer from nervous and mental illness everywhere on earth may be helped and consoled. I recommend to You in particular *(here mention those you wish to pray for).*

Be pleased to hear the prayers of Saint Dymphna and of your Blessed Mother. Give the sick and afflicted the consolation they need and especially the cure they so desire, if it be your will. O God, through Saint Dymphna, grant relief to those who suffer from mental afflictions and nervous disorders. Through Christ our Lord. Amen.

Feast Day: May 15

Prayer for
Motherhood

O glorious Saint Gerard,
powerful intercessor before God,
and wonder worker of our day,
I call upon you and seek your
help. You who always fulfilled
God's will on earth, help me to
do God's holy will. Intercede
with the Giver of life, from
whom all parenthood proceeds,
that I may conceive and raise
children who will please God
in this life, and be heirs to the
kingdom of heaven. Amen.

Prayer to
Saint Peregrine

God, who gave Saint Peregrine
an angel as his companion, the
Mother of God as his teacher,
and Jesus as the physician for his
illness; grant, we ask you, that
we on earth may intensely love
the Blessed Virgin Mary and our
Savior, and in heaven bless them
forever. Grant that we receive
the favor for which we now ask
through Jesus Christ our Lord.
Amen.

*One Our Father, Hail Mary and Glory Be
accompanied by: Saint Peregrine, pray for us.*

Saint Peregrine is recognized as
the patron of cancer victims
because a malignant cancerous
growth on his leg was cured.

An Act of Consecration to Our Lady of the Miraculous Medal

O Virgin Mother of God, Mary Immaculate, we dedicate and consecrate ourselves to you under the title of Our Lady of the Miraculous Medal.

May this medal be for each one of us a sure sign of your affection for us and a constant reminder of our duties toward you.

Ever while wearing it, may we be blessed by your loving protection and preserved in the grace of your Son.

O most powerful Virgin, Mother of our Savior, keep us close to you every moment of our lives.

Obtain for us, your children, the grace of a happy death; so that, in union with you, we may enjoy the bliss of heaven forever. Amen.

O Mary, conceived without sin, pray for us who have recourse to you.
(3 times)

The Memorare

Remember, O most gracious
Virgin Mary,
that never was it known that
anyone who fled to your
protection,
implored your help,
or sought your intercession
was left unaided.

Inspired by this confidence,
we come to you,
O Virgin of virgins,
our Mother!

To you we come,
before you we stand,
sinful and sorrowful.

O Mother of the Word incarnate,
despise not our petitions, but
in your mercy hear and answer us.

Amen.

The Hail Mary

Hail Mary, full of grace,
the Lord is with you.

Blessed are you
among women,
and blessed is the fruit
of your womb, Jesus.

Holy Mary,
Mother of God,
pray for us sinners,
now and at the hour
of our death.

Amen.

I Said A Prayer
For You Today

I said a prayer for you today
And know God must have heard.
I felt the answer in my heart
Although he spoke no word!

I didn't ask for wealth or fame
(I knew you wouldn't mind).
I asked him to send treasures
Of a far more lasting kind!

I asked that he'd be near you
At the start of each new day;
To grant you health and blessings
And friends to share your way!

I asked for happiness for you
In all things great and small.
But it was for his loving care
I prayed the most of all!

Cross in My Pocket

I carry a cross in my pocket
A simple reminder to me
Of the fact that I am a Christian
No matter where I may be.

This little cross is not magic
Nor is it a good luck charm.
It isn't meant to protect me
From every physical harm.

It's not for identification
For all the world to see.
It's simply an understanding
Between my Savior and me.

When I put my hand in my pocket
To bring out a coin or key.
The cross is there to remind me
Of the price he paid for me.

It reminds me, too, to be thankful
For my blessings day by day
And to strive to serve him better
In all that I do and say.

It's also a daily reminder
Of the peace and comfort I share
With all who know my master
And give themselves to his care.

So, I carry a cross in my pocket
Reminding no one but me
That Jesus Christ is Lord of my life
If only I'll let him be.

Footprints

One night a man had a dream. He dreamed he was walking along the beach with the LORD. Across the sky flashed scenes from his life. For each scene, he noticed two sets of footprints in the sand; one belonging to him, and the other to the LORD.

When the last scene of his life flashed before him, he looked back at the footprints in the sand. He noticed that many times along the path of his life there was only one set of footprints. He also noticed that it happened at the very lowest and saddest times in his life.

This really bothered him and he questioned the LORD about it. "LORD, you said that once I decided to follow you, you'd walk with me all the way. But I have noticed that during the most troublesome times in my life, there is only one set of footprints; I don't understand why when I needed you most you would leave me."

The LORD replied, "My precious, precious child, I love you and I would never leave you. During your times of trial and suffering, when you see only one set of footprints, it was then that I carried you."

Author: Margaret Fishback Powers © 1964

Serenity Prayer

God, grant me the courage to change the things I can change, the serenity to accept those I cannot change, and the wisdom to know the difference. But God, grant me the courage not to give up on what I think is right, even though I think it is hopeless.

The Apostles' Creed

I believe in God, the Father almighty, Creator of heaven and earth.

I believe in Jesus Christ, his only Son, our Lord. He was conceived by the power of the Holy Spirit and born of the Virgin Mary. He suffered under Pontius Pilate, was crucified, died, and was buried. He descended to the dead. On the third day he rose again. He ascended into heaven, and is seated at the right hand of the Father. He will come again to judge the living and the dead.

I believe in the Holy Spirit, the holy catholic Church, the communion of saints, the forgiveness of sins, the resurrection of the body, and life everlasting. Amen.

Prayer for the Helpless Unborn

Heavenly Father, in your love for us, protect against the wickedness of the devil, those helpless little ones to whom you have given the gift of life.

Touch with pity the hearts of those women pregnant in our world today who are not thinking of motherhood.

Help them to see that the child they carry is made in your image – as well as theirs – made for eternal life.

Dispel their fear and selfishness and give them true womanly hearts to love their babies and give them birth and all the needed care that a mother alone can give.

We ask this through Jesus Christ, your Son, our Lord, who lives and reigns with You and the Holy Spirit, one God, forever and ever. Amen.

Feast Day: December 12

Police Officer's Prayer to Saint Michael

Saint Michael, heaven's glorious commissioner of police, who once so neatly and successfully cleared God's premises of all its undesirables, look with kindly and professional eyes on your earthly force.

Give us cool heads, stout hearts, an uncanny flair for investigation and wise judgment.

Make us the terror of burglars, the friend of children and law-abiding citizens, kind to strangers, polite to bores, strict with lawbreakers and impervious to temptations.

You know, Saint Michael, from your own experiences with the devil that the police officer's lot on earth is not always a happy one; but your sense of duty that so pleased God, your hard knocks that so surprised the devil, and your angelic self-control give us inspiration.

And when we lay down our night sticks, enroll us in your heavenly force, where we will be as proud to guard the throne of God as we have been to guard the city of all the people. Amen.

Feast Day: September 29

Prayer for Safe Delivery

O great Saint Gerard, beloved servant of Jesus Christ, perfect imitator of your meek and humble Savior, and devoted child of the Mother of God, enkindle within my heart one spark of that heavenly fire of charity which glowed in your heart and made you an angel of love.

O glorious Saint Gerard, because when falsely accused of crime, you did bear, like your Divine Master, without murmur or complaint, the calumnies of wicked men, you have been raised up by God as the patron and protector of expectant mothers.

Preserve me from danger and from the excessive pains accompanying childbirth, and shield the child which I now carry, that it may see the light of day and receive the purifying and life-giving waters of baptism through Jesus Christ our Lord. Amen.

(Nine Hail Marys)

Feast Day: October 16

The Motorist's Prayer

Grant me, O Lord, a steady hand
and watchful eye.

That no one shall be hurt as I pass by.

You gave life, I pray no act of mine
May take away or mar that gift of thine.

Shelter those, dear Lord
who bear my company,

From the evils of fire and all calamity.

Teach me, to use my car for others need;

Nor miss through love of undue speed

The beauty of the world; that thus I may

With joy and courtesy go on my way.

Saint Christopher, holy patron of
travelers,

Protect me and lead me safely
to my destiny.

Prayer to Saint Anne

O God, you bestowed on Saint Anne such grace that she was found worthy to become the mother of Mary, who brought forth your only begotten Son.

Grant that we may be helped by her intercession.

(Here make your request)

Prayer to Saint Barbara, Virgin and Martyr

Saint Barbara, dedicated to Christ, suffered martyrdom in 235 or 238. The location of her death is unknown. Her legendary story tells us her father was a rich heathen called Dioscorus. Upon professing the faith, she and Saint Juliana were martyred together.

O God, who among the other miracles of your power, have given Barbara, your virgin ever faithful, the victory of martyrdom, grant, we beg you, that we, who are celebrating the heavenly birthday of Blessed Barbara, your virgin and martyr, may, by her example, draw nearer to you. Amen.

Prayer in Honor of Saint Lucy

O God, our creator and redeemer, mercifully hear our prayers that as we venerate your servant, Saint Lucy, for the light of faith You bestowed upon her, You promise to increase and preserve this same light in our souls, that we may be able to avoid evil, to do good and to abhor nothing so much as the blindness and the darkness of evil and of sin.

Relying on your goodness, O God, we humbly ask you, by the intercession of your servant, Saint Lucy, that you would give perfect vision to our eyes, that they may serve for your greater honor and glory, and for the salvation of our souls in this world, that we may come to the enjoyment of the unfailing light of the Lamb of God in paradise.

Saint Lucy, virgin and martyr, hear our prayers and obtain our petitions.

Feast Day: December 13

Prayer to Saint Rita

O God, who communicated so great grace to Saint Rita that she imitated your example in the love of enemies and bore in her heart and on her countenance the sacred marks of your love and passion: grant, we beg you, by her merits and intercession, that we may love our enemies and ever contemplate with deep contrition the sorrows of your passion: who lives and reigns world without end. Amen.

A plenary indulgence on the usual conditions, if the daily recitation of this prayer is continued for a month.

Firefighter's Prayer

Almighty God, protector of all, your strength, power, and wisdom are a beacon of light to all:

Give special guidance to firefighters so that we may be protected from harm while performing our duty.

Help me with your loving care while I work to save the lives and property of all people, young and old.

Give me the courage, the alertness to protect my neighbors and all others whom I am pledged to aid when involved in fire or accident. Amen.

Prayer to Obtain the Glorification of Padre Pio

O Jesus, full of grace and charity, victim for sinners, so impelled by your love of us that you willed to die on the cross, I humbly entreat you to glorify in heaven and on earth, the servant of God, Padre Pio of Pietrelcina, who generously participated in your sufferings, who loved you so much and labored so faithfully for the glory of your heavenly Father and for the good of souls.

With confidence, I beg you to grant me, through his intercession, the grace of...which I ardently desire.

3 times: Glory Be to the Father...

Imprimatur: Manfredonia, 12-3-1971

+ Valentino Vailati, Archbishop

Prayer to
Saint Benedict

God our Father, you made
Saint Benedict an outstanding
guide to teach men how to live
in your service.

Grant that by preferring your
love to everything else, we
may walk in the way of your
commandments.

Through Christ our Lord. Amen.

A Nurse's Prayer

O my God, teach me to receive the sick in your name. Give to my efforts success for the glory of your holy name.

It is your work: without you, I cannot succeed.

Grant that the sick you have placed in my care may be abundantly blessed, and not one of them be lost because of any neglect on my part.

Help me to overcome, every temporal weakness, and strengthen in me whatever may enable me to bring joy to the lives of those I serve.

Give me grace, for the sake of your sick ones and of those lives that will be influenced by them. Amen.

Teacher's Prayer

I want to teach my students how
To live this life on earth,
To face its struggles and its strife
And improve their worth.
Not just the lesson in a book
Or how the rivers flow,
But how to choose the proper path
Wherever they may go.
To understand eternal truth
And know the right from wrong
And gather all the beauty of
A flower and a song.
For if I help the world to grow
In wisdom and in grace
Then I shall feel that I have won
And I have filled my place.
And so I ask your guidance, God
That I may do my part
For character and confidence
And happiness of heart.

Healing Prayer
at Bedtime

Lord Jesus, through the power of the Holy Spirit, go back into my memory as I sleep.

Every hurt that has ever been done to me, heal that hurt.

Every hurt that I have ever caused another person, heal that hurt.

All the relationships that have been damaged in my whole life
that I am not aware of, heal those relationships.

But, Lord, if there is anything that I need to do,

If I need to go to a person
because he or she is still suffering
from my hand,bring to my awareness
that person. I choose to forgive, and
I ask to be forgiven.

Remove whatever bitterness
may be in my heart, Lord,
and fill the empty spaces with your love. Amen.